What's the difference between . . .

Apes and Monkeys
and Other Living Things?

Now available in Wiley's *What's the Difference?* Series:

What's the Difference Between Lenses and Prisms and Other Scientific Things?
   by Gary Soucie

What's the Difference Between Apes and Monkeys and Other Living Things?
   by Gary Soucie

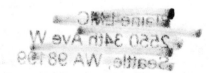

What's the difference between . . .
Apes and Monkeys
and Other Living Things?

Gary Soucie

Illustrated by Jeff Domm

John Wiley & Sons, Inc.
New York • Chichester • Brisbane • Toronto • Singapore

For Pam-I-Am's Sam-I-Am:
Samuel Leroy Starr
a curious lad

© 1995 by Gary A. Soucie
Published by John Wiley & Sons, Inc.
Illustrations © 1995 by Jeff Domm

This publication is designed to provide accurate and authoritative information in regard
to the subject matter covered. It is sold with the understanding that the publisher is not
engaged in rendering professional services. If legal, accounting, medical, psychological,
or any other expert assistance is required, the services of a competent professional person
should be sought.

Library of Congress Cataloging-in-Publication Data

Soucie, Gary.
    What's the difference between apes and monkeys and other living
  things?/Gary Soucie; illustrated by Jeff Domm.
        p.   cm.
    Includes index.
    ISBN 0-471-08625-8   (paper; alk. paper)
      1. Animals—Miscellanea—Juvenile literature.   2. Plants—
  —Miscellanea—Juvenile literature.   [1. Animals—Miscellanea.
  2. Plants—Miscellanea.   3. Questions and answers.]   I. Domm, Jeff,
  1958–   ill.   II. Title.
  QH48,S648   1995
  574—dc20   95-6585
                                                                  AC

Printed in the United States of America

10   9   8   7   6   5   4   3   2   1

Contents

About This Book   vii

Plants   1

What's the difference between
Grasses and Weeds?   2

What's the difference between
Blossoms and Flowers?   4

What's the difference between
Pollen and Spores?   6

What's the difference between
Petals and Sepals?   8

What's the difference between
Stalks and Stems?   10

What's the difference between
Leaves and Leaflets?   12

What's the difference between
Trees and Shrubs?   14

What's the difference between
Evergreens and Conifers?   16

What's the difference between
Redwoods and Sequoias?   18

What's the difference between
Poison Ivy and Poison Oak?   20

What's the difference between
Goldenrod and Ragweed?   22

What's the difference between
Fruits and Berries?   24

What's the difference between
Fruits and Nuts?   26

What's the difference between
Roots, Tubers, and Bulbs?   28

What's the difference between
Lilies and Orchids?   30

What's the difference between
Reeds and Rushes?   32

What's the difference between
Anemones and Sea Anemones?   34

What's the difference between
Mushrooms and Toadstools?   36

What's the difference between
Mosses and Lichens?   38

What's the difference between
Molds and Mildews?   40

Animals 43

What's the difference between
Apes and Monkeys?   44

What's the difference between
Jaguars and Leopards?   46

What's the difference between
Horns and Antlers?   48

What's the difference between
Rabbits and Hares?   50

What's the difference between
Dolphins, Porpoises,
and Whales?   52

What's the difference between
Seals and Sea Lions?   54

What's the difference between
Hair and Fur?   56

What's the difference between
Ducks and Geese?   58

What's the difference between
Reptiles and Amphibians?   60

What's the difference between
Newts and Salamanders?   62

What's the difference between
Frogs and Toads?   64

What's the difference between
Alligators and Crocodiles?   66

What's the difference between
Turtles, Tortoises,
and Terrapins?   68

What's the difference between
Skates and Stingrays?   70

What's the difference between
Bone and Cartilage?   72

What's the difference between
Octopuses and Squid?   74

What's the difference between
Butterflies and Moths?   76

What's the difference between
Bugs and Insects?   78

What's the difference between
Bees, Wasps, and Hornets?   80

What's the difference between
Crickets and Grasshoppers?   82

Glossary   84
Index   87

About This Book

This book looks at the differences between lots of things in the world of plants and animals that many people tend to confuse. Sometimes the differences between things are small, and easily overlooked, but every distinction is important to scientists.

How This Book Works

The book is divided into two sections. The first answers questions about plants. The second covers animals.

As an example of how each entry is set up, let's begin with this question:

What's the difference between . . .
Plants and Animals?

What do you mean, "Too easy"? Sure, it's easy to tell the difference between a rabbit and a carrot, but what makes one an animal and the other a plant? Even scientists aren't sure exactly where the line should be drawn. Here are the rules (and some exceptions) that scientists use to distinguish between the Plant and Animal Kingdoms:

- Plants have a green substance, called **chlorophyll**, that enables them to turn sunlight into food. Animals don't. (However, mushrooms and other fungi don't have chlorophyll, and they aren't animals.)
- Plants have rigid walls separating their cells, and animals have flexible cell membranes.
- Animals can move from place to place, and plants can't. (But what about sponges, corals, barnacles, and other animals that spend their lives rooted to a single spot? And what about single-celled algae and other primitive plants that move all about their watery homes?)
- Animals have a nervous system, and plants don't. (However, the animals called **hydras**—which are sort of like a freshwater jellyfish—have nerves, but no system to control them. And some plants have groups of cells that enable them to respond quickly to their environment, almost as if they had nerves. For example, if you touch a mimosa tree's branch, the leaves will quickly close up.)

No wonder my dictionary of biology does not have entries for "plant" or "animal." Drawing the line between the plant and animal kingdoms is one of biology's biggest challenges.

Did you know?

- Many biologists now recognize three more kingdoms of living things. The most primitive one-celled organisms, such as bacteria and blue-green algae, now belong to the **Monera Kingdom**. Most other one-celled organisms (amoebas, euglenas, paramecia, diatoms, and the rest of the algae) belong to the **Protist Kingdom**. **Fungi** (mushrooms, yeasts, molds, slime molds, and related organisms) have their own kingdom.

- Scientists aren't sure viruses belong to any of the kingdoms of living things.

Okay, now you know how it works.

You might have noticed that a few words in this book—such as **chlorophyll** in our example—are printed in **boldface**. Just in case you don't know these words, they are defined in a glossary at the end of the book. Using this book is easier than going to a dictionary or encyclopedia, but you should refer to them often whenever you are wondering about plants and animals.

You can read this book from cover to cover, dip into it at random, or look up specific things you want to know about. You can also use it as a game to play with family and friends. Just read the questions aloud and see whether anyone knows the answers. And don't forget the *Did you know?* questions.

If you want to keep score, award points for correct answers. A straightforward question that has a single answer could be worth one, five, ten, or however many points you want to use. If the answer is a list of things, you can award a single point for each correct response.

If you have a lot of people in the game, you might divide them into teams of two, three, or four and let them compete for points. You can ask questions of each player (or team) in turn, or you can throw the question out and let the player who first raises a hand, rings a bell, or shouts, "I know!" have the first shot at it. You've watched game shows on television. You know the different ways to do it.

However you decide to use this book, I hope you learn a lot of neat things and have a lot of fun. I did while writing it.

Plants

What's the difference . . .
Grasses and Weeds?

Weeds are any plants that are useless to humankind, have little economic value, or simply are growing where you don't want them.

Grasses are green plants with long, slender leaves that grow in two vertical rows on opposite sides of a jointed stem. As a result, the plant looks like a split tube.

CLOSE-UP OF GRASS

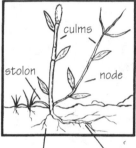

culms

stolon

node

roots

rhizome

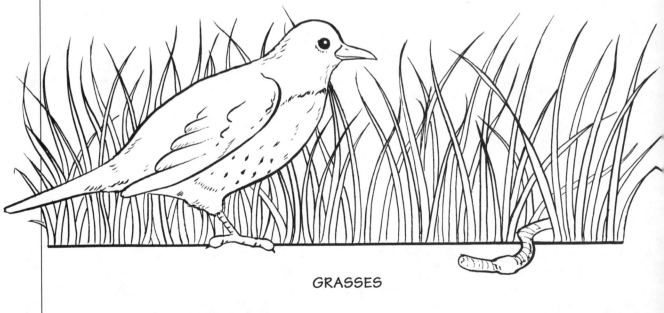

GRASSES

2

Grasses also produce small, dry, one-seeded fruits that are sometimes arranged in clusters.

Even though the difference between grasses and weeds are clear, people often misuse the terms. If it grows in their lawns, and if people are willing to mow it, they probably call it grass. (Unfortunately, quite a few weeds also grow in lawns, such as dandelions, crabgrass, and chickweed.) If grazing animals will eat it, it's also probably called grass. Many aquatic (water) plants are called weeds, especially seaweeds. So are the leafy parts of some herbs, such as dillweed.

Did you know?

- Most of the valuable cereal grains—corn, wheat, oats, rice, barley, rye, and wild rice—are grasses.

- Sugarcane is a grass. So is sorghum, which looks like a cross between corn and sugarcane. Sorghum is grown in America for animal fodder. In many other countries, sorghum is also used for grain and to make syrup.

- Bamboos and canes—which are grasses—flower only once every 40 to 50 years.

WEEDS

What's the difference between . . .
Blossoms and Flowers?

Flowers are the reproductive structures of certain seed-bearing plants called flowering plants. Blossoms are *showy flowers*, the kind we grow in our gardens because they are pretty to look at. Grasses are flowering plants, for example, but people never talk about grass blossoms.

Mostly, when we think of flowers, we think of their pretty petals. But flowers also include specific parts that are directly involved in reproduction.

The **stamen** is the male reproductive organ. Flowers usually have several stamens. In a typical flower, stamens have long stalks. On top of each stamen is an **anther**. The anthers produce the pollen that fertilizes the female organs.

BLOSSOMS

4

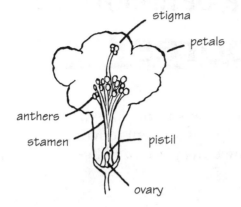

PARTS OF A FLOWER

stigma

petals

anthers

stamen

pistil

ovary

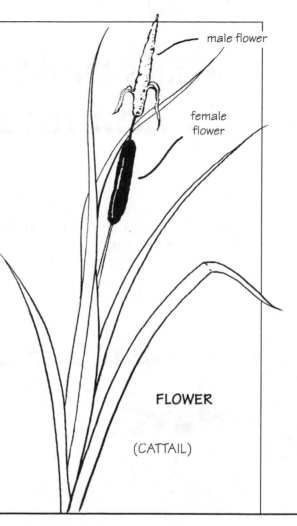

male flower

female flower

FLOWER

(CATTAIL)

The **pistil** (or **carpel**) is the flower's female organ. A flower may have just one pistil, or several. At the tip of the pistil is the **stigma**, which collects the pollen. The stigma has a sticky surface, so the pollen will cling to it.

The **ovary**, a part of the pistil, is the flower's real reproductive factory. Inside the ovary are one or more tiny bodies called **ovules**. Each ovule contains an egg cell.

Some plants have both male and female parts in the same flowers. Others produce two kinds of flowers—male and female—on the same plant. Still others produce male and female flowers on different plants. For more on how plants reproduce, see the next section.

Did you know?
- Bee orchids attract male bees by producing flowers that look and smell like female bees. If no bees come around, the bee orchid's stamens bend over and transfer the pollen themselves.

What's the difference between . . .
Pollen and Spores?

Pollen is the name of the tiny reproductive grains formed by the
male parts (stamens) of flowering plants. Spores are reproductive
bodies that become detached from nonflowering plants and become new plants.

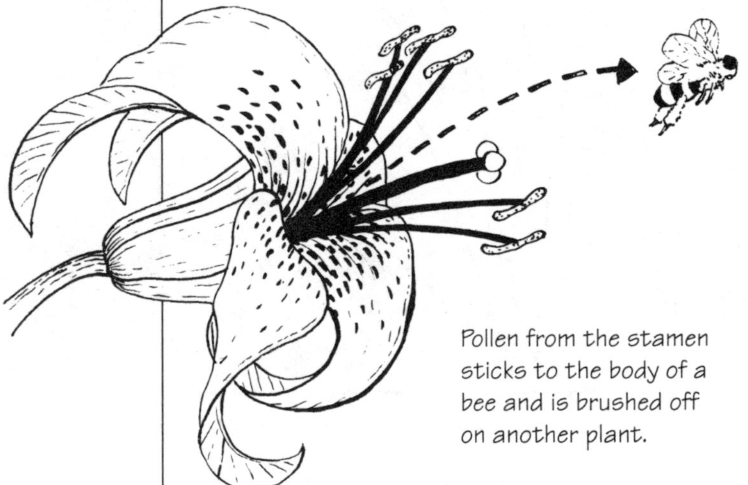

Pollen from the stamen
sticks to the body of a
bee and is brushed off
on another plant.

POLLEN

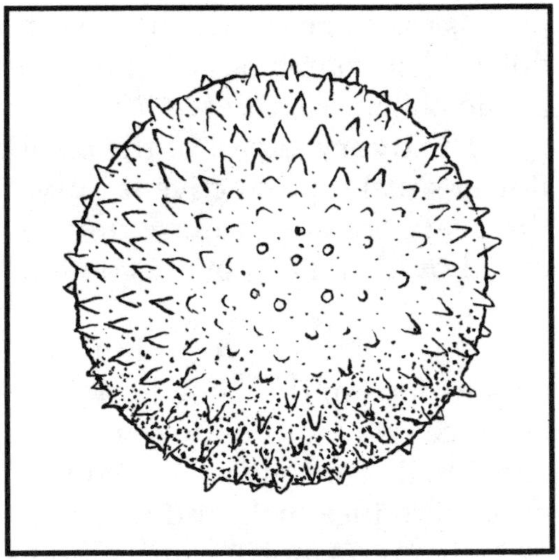

CLOSE-UP OF POLLEN

SPORES

In some nonflowering plants, spores produced by parent plants become new plants quickly and directly. This process is called asexual reproduction, because you only need one parent plant.

In seed-producing plants, pollen from the male part of a plant fertilizes the ovaries of the female part of a plant. These fertilized ovaries produce the seeds that become the new plants. This is called sexual reproduction because you need both a male and a female parent. Even in plants that pollinate themselves, both male and female parts are needed.

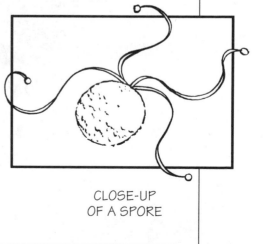

CLOSE-UP
OF A SPORE

7

What's the difference between . . .
Petals and Sepals?

Petals are the delicate structures that surround a flower's reproductive organs. Sepals are the leafy-looking structures that surround and protect a flower bud before it opens.

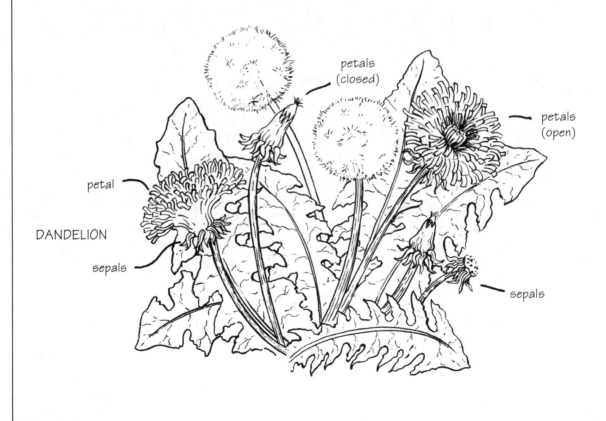

petals (closed)

petals (open)

petal

DANDELION

sepals

sepals

Petals are often brightly colored and scented to attract pollinating insects. Some petals also produce a sweet liquid called nectar, which insects like to eat. The nectar collects in a group of cells at the base of the petal, called a nectary.

Sepals are usually green, but on some flowers they are colored. On some plants, the sepals wither and fall off after the flower opens. In others, they stay on the plant and form a ring around the opened petals.

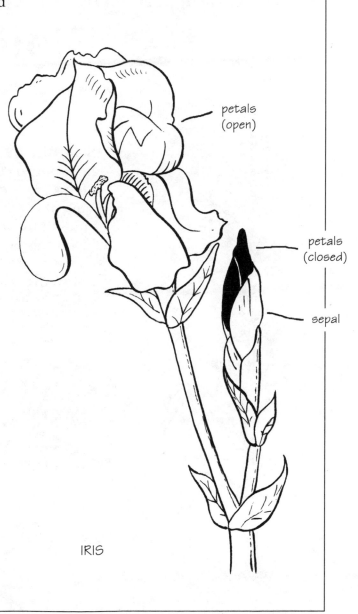

petals (open)

petals (closed)

sepal

IRIS

What's the difference between . . .
Stalks and Stems?

Stalks are the long, usually thin, structures that hold flowers, leaves, and other parts of a plant. Stems are the main stalks of only vascular plants. **Vascular** plants have the ability to carry water and sap to various parts of the plant. Stems can be found on trees, roses, and grasses, which are all vascular plants. Plants that have stalks, but not stems, such as mushrooms and mosses, are called **nonvascular** plants.

DON'T STEP ON THE STALKS.

STALKS

Also, the word "stalk" is usually used only for nonwoody plants. In other words, a tree trunk is a stem, but it isn't a stalk. People often call twigs, flower stalks, leaf stalks, and other plant parts stems, but they really aren't.

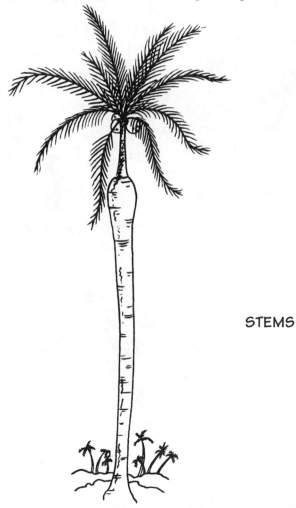

STEMS

Did you know?

- A flower stalk is also called a peduncle. The word comes from the Latin and means "little foot."

11

What's the difference between . . .
Leaves and Leaflets?

Leaflets are small leaves that grow from the same stalk.

Leaves are a plant's food-making organs. Most leaves contain a green substance called **chlorophyll**. Chlorophyll helps plants to make food out of sunlight, water, and carbon dioxide. Plants also need oxygen to convert food into the energy they need to grow. Leaves take in the carbon dioxide and oxygen a plant needs.

maple leaf

SIMPLE LEAVES

cattail
leaf

A leaf that has just one leaf blade is called a simple leaf. Maples, cattails, and dandelions have simple leaves. One that has several leaflets is a compound leaf. Walnuts, clovers, and most ferns have compound leaves.

Did you know?

- The very first leaves produced by seeds are called cotyledons. Cotyledons seldom look like the rest of the plant's leaves. Often, they look more like tiny Ping-Pong paddles.

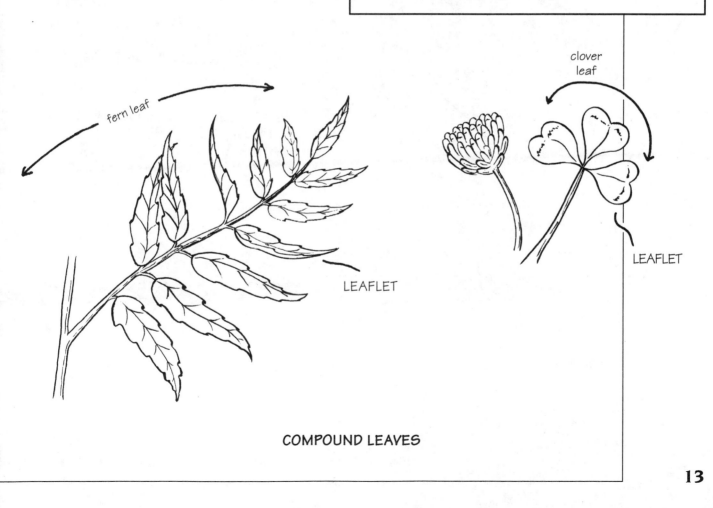

fern leaf

clover leaf

LEAFLET

LEAFLET

COMPOUND LEAVES

13

What's the difference between . . .
Trees and Shrubs?

The important difference is in their woody stems. Shrubs have several. Trees usually have a single stem, or trunk.

To be called a tree, a woody plant must be at least 20 feet tall when fully grown. Shrubs are usually shorter than that.

TREE

14

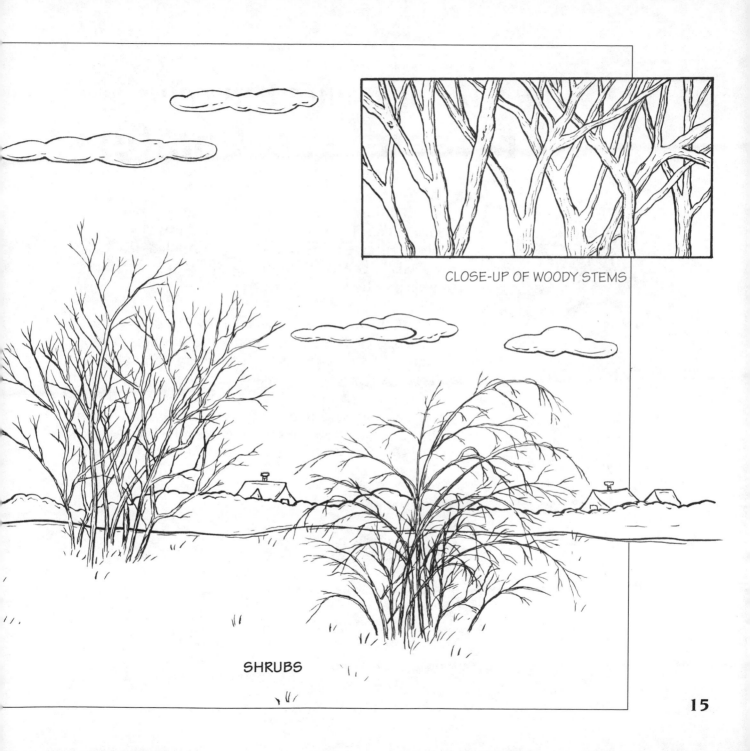

CLOSE-UP OF WOODY STEMS

SHRUBS

15

What's the difference between . . .
Evergreens and Conifers?

Plants that don't lose their leaves in winter are ever-greens, even if they are lush tropical plants. Trees or large shrubs that have narrow, pointed, needlelike leaves and bear seeds in cones are conifers. (The word "conifer" comes from the word "cone.")

Conifers include such well-known trees as pines, spruces, firs, cypresses, redwoods, and junipers. The standard Christmas tree is both an evergreen and a conifer. Perhaps that's why so many people think the words have the same meaning. Yews are also considered conifers, even though they don't bear cones. Some yews have seeds that protrude from red, jellylike cups that look like berries. Other yews have large, nutlike seeds that are

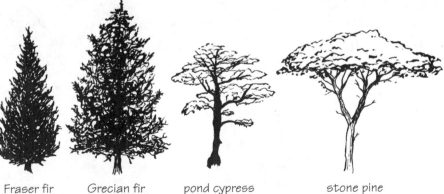

black spruce   Fraser fir   Grecian fir   pond cypress   stone pine

CONIFERS

16

completely enclosed in fruits that re-semble plums.

Larches, or tamaracks, are conifers, but they are **deciduous** rather than evergreen. Their needles turn yellow and drop off in the fall.

Okay, then, let's review. Some evergreens are conifers, but many evergreens are not. And some conifers are not evergreens. A few conifers don't even bear cones. Aren't you glad you asked?

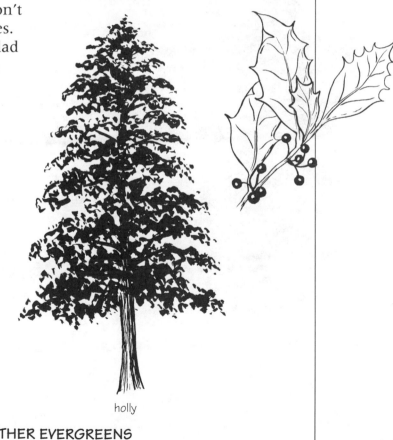

Chusan palm

holly

OTHER EVERGREENS

What's the difference between . . .
Redwoods and Sequoias?

Both the coast redwood of the California coast and the giant sequoia of that state's Sierra Nevada mountains are actually sequoias. But they thrive in quite different climates.

The coast redwood grows tall and straight in foggy, rainy climates at fairly low elevations. It is the tallest living thing in the world. The tallest redwood measures more than 369 feet.

The giant sequoia lives in higher, drier places. It doesn't grow as tall as its coastal cousin (the tallest one measured *only* 310 feet), but it grows much

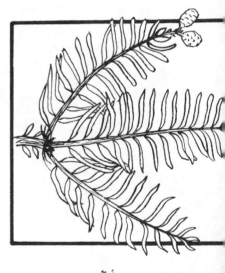

REDWOOD

bigger around. In fact, it's the *largest* living thing on earth. The General Sherman Tree in Sequoia National Part is estimated to weigh more than 6,000 tons. (The largest living animal, the blue whale, weighs less than 200 tons.) The General Grant Tree nearby is the world's thickest tree; its trunk is more than 40 feet in diameter at the base.

Did *you know*?

- Coast redwoods can live as long as 2,200 years, and giant sequoias, more than 3,500. Only the bristlecone pine—also a tree of the Sierra Nevada—lives longer, about 4,000 years.

SEQUOIA

What's the difference between . . .
Poison Ivy and Poison Oak?

These closely related plants are very similar: both have leaves with three leaflets, produce greenish-white berries, and contain a toxic oil that irritates the skin. But there are several differences.

Poison ivy grows all over the country, but real poison oak only grows in the Southwest and on the Pacific Coast.

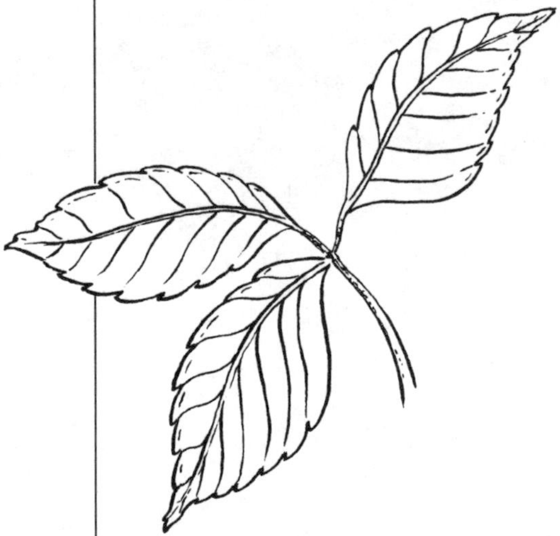

POISON IVY

20

Poison ivy leaflets may be smooth-edged, toothed, notched, or lobed. Poison oak leaflets are always notched or lobed.

Poison oak usually grows as a shrub (only occasionally as a vine) to 9 feet tall. Poison ivy commonly grows in different forms: as a shrub or a vine, sometimes even as a small tree. Poison ivy vines can climb trees to 100 feet or more.

POISON OAK

What's the difference between . . .
Goldenrod and Ragweed?

The ragweed plant is responsible for hay fever. The goldenrod plant usually is not.

Goldenrod has been wrongly accused by hay fever victims for a long time. Because they are so tall (as tall as 8 feet) and have large, golden-yellow flowerheads, golden-rods get noticed. At the height of the hay fever season, golden-rods are the most

I DIDN'T DO IT!

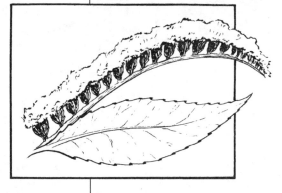

GOLDENROD

prominent "weeds" in bloom. As a result, they get blamed for causing all the sneezing, runny eyes, and headaches. But goldenrod pollen is too heavy to blow in the wind, so it's unlikely anyone ever suffered from hay fever because of it.

Ragweeds are more likely responsible for the suffering. They're also tall (giant ragweed can grow to 15 feet!), but they aren't as easily noticed as goldenrod. That's because their flowers are small and dull-colored. But ragweeds release tons of pollen into the air. If you look at a grain of ragweed pollen under a microscope, you'll see why they cause such misery. Each grain is covered with tiny barbed hooks that attach themselves to human **bronchial** tissue and won't let go.

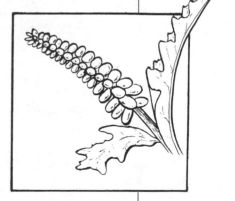

RAGWEED

23

What's the difference between . . .
Fruits and Berries?

Fruits are the ripened, seed-bearing ovaries of flowers. Berries are a particular kind of fruit.

Berries contain more than one seed, a fleshy pulp, and an outer skin. Blueberries, raspberries, and blackberries are examples of true berries.

FRUIT SALAD
1 apple
1 banana
¼ cup of peas
1 orange
1 peach
1 eggplant
2 tomatoes

FRUITS

24

blackberries

blueberries

Did you know?

- Tomatoes, eggplants, squashes, peas, beans, and corn are actually fruits. If it develops from a flower's ovary and has seeds, it's a fruit, even if you wouldn't want to eat it for dessert. We mostly use the word "fruit" for those fruits that taste sweet (except for citrus fruits such as lemons and limes, which aren't very sweet).

- The watermelon is a berry. So are pomegranates, kiwis, grapes, and bananas. They are berries because they have outer skins, fleshy pulps, and lots of seeds.

- The strawberry isn't a berry at all. It's really the pulpy center of a flower related to the rose family. The tiny "seeds" on the outside of a strawberry are actually complete, one-seeded fruits.

raspberries

grapes

BERRIES

What's the difference between . . .
Fruits and Nuts?

Nuts are actually single-seeded fruits. But unlike apples or oranges, nuts have hard shells and a dry flesh. Nuts also do not open when they are ripe. Common types of nuts include acorns, chestnuts, filberts (another name for hazelnuts), and beechnuts.

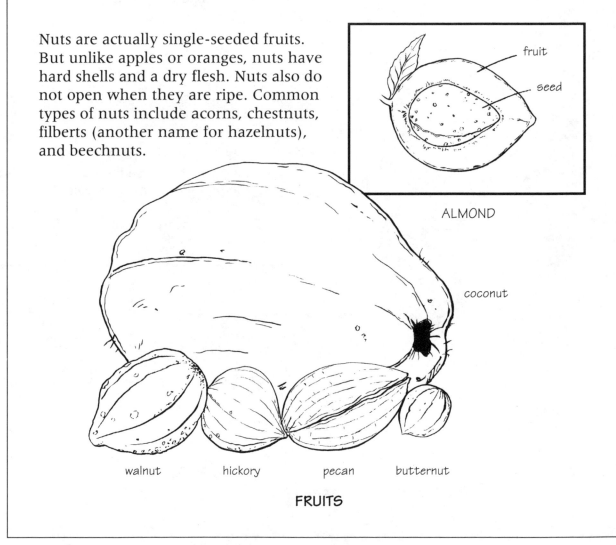

fruit

seed

ALMOND

coconut

walnut   hickory   pecan   butternut

FRUITS

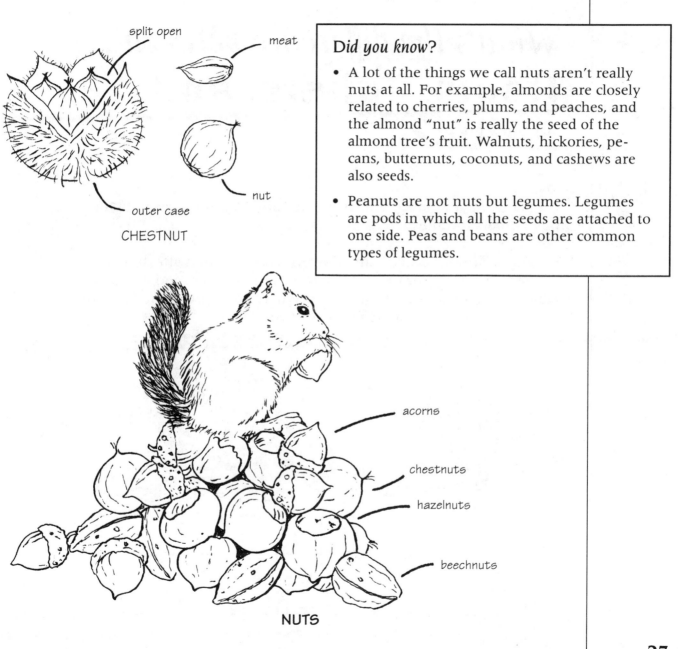

split open

meat

nut

outer case

CHESTNUT

Did you know?

- A lot of the things we call nuts aren't really nuts at all. For example, almonds are closely related to cherries, plums, and peaches, and the almond "nut" is really the seed of the almond tree's fruit. Walnuts, hickories, pecans, butternuts, coconuts, and cashews are also seeds.

- Peanuts are not nuts but legumes. Legumes are pods in which all the seeds are attached to one side. Peas and beans are other common types of legumes.

acorns

chestnuts

hazelnuts

beechnuts

NUTS

What's the difference between . . .
Roots, Tubers, and Bulbs?

All plants have roots of some sort. But only certain types of plants have tubers or bulbs.

Roots are the leafless and flowerless organs that attach plants to the earth, trees, or rocks. Most roots are underground, but some plants have air roots. But no matter where roots grow, they absorb food and water to help the plant survive.

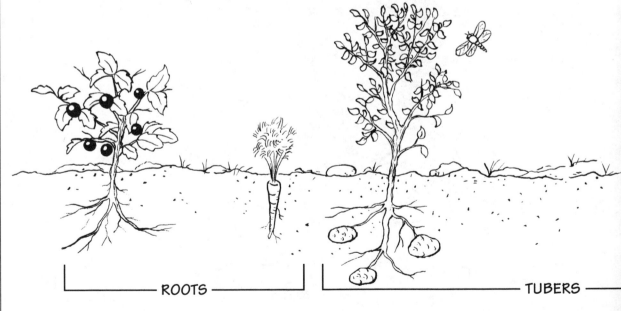

ROOTS ——— TUBERS ———

Tubers and bulbs are both reproductive organs that produce buds. Because they produce buds, they can produce new plants. Roots don't produce buds.

Tubers are swollen, underground stems that store food. Oxalis and cyclamen are just two of the many plants that have tubers.

Bulbs are short, thick, underground stems. Each of these stems is surrounded by layers of scaly leaves that store food for the plant. Tulips, hyacinths, and many lilies all develop from bulbs.

Many roots, bulbs, and tubers are good to eat. Carrots, radishes, and turnips all have edible roots. As for the edible underground parts of other plants, potatoes and yams are tubers, while onions and garlic are bulbs.

Did you know?

- Sweet potatoes and yams are not the same. They aren't even closely related. Yams are tubers, while sweet potatoes are edible roots. What is called a yam in the United States is just a variety of sweet potato.

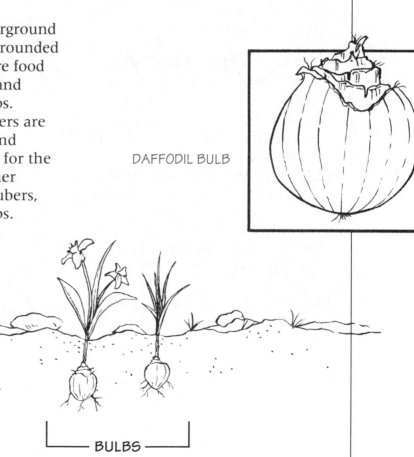

DAFFODIL BULB

BULBS

What's the difference between . . .
Lilies and Orchids?

Lilies and orchids look similar, but they are actually very different plants.

Because both plants often have such pretty, showy flowers, some people get them confused. But one look at the flower will tell you which it is, if you know what to look for. Like most flowers, lilies have blossoms that are perfectly **symmetrical** (which means they are the same on all sides, top and bottom, left and right). But the flowers of orchids are symmetrical the way people are: The left and

LILIES

right sides are alike, but the top and bottom are very different. Most orchids have a large "lip" at the bottom of the flower.

If you sniff the flowers, you may notice another difference. Many orchids smell sweet. Very few lilies have any smell at all. Orchids and lilies also differ in the way their reproductive organs are arranged. Lilies have six stamens. Orchids have one or two. In lilies, the ovary is inside the flower. In orchids, it's below the flower's petals.

Did you know?

- Orchid seeds contain no nutrients and cannot develop until they have been "infected" by a certain type of fungus. The developing plant feeds on the fungus until it establishes its own roots.

- Asparagus and the so-called asparagus fern (it's really an asparagus, not a fern) are both lilies.

- Onions, garlics, and leeks are also kinds of lilies. Many other lilies that look like onions or garlics, but do not have their smell, are poisonous.

- Utah chose the sego lily as its state flower because the plant's bulbs kept the state's first settlers from starving to death when swarms of insects devoured their crops.

ORCHIDS

What's the difference between . . .
Reeds and Rushes?

Reeds are tall grasses with jointed stems, broad leaves, and large plumes on top. Rushes are marsh plants with unjointed stems, sharply pointed tubular leaves, and tiny, three-petaled flowers.

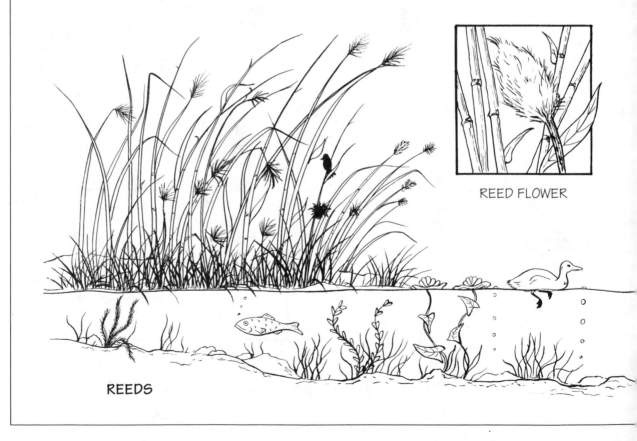

REED FLOWER

REEDS

People often use either word to mean any of the tall, thin plants that grow in marshes and around other bodies of water. The straight, hollow stems of many of these marsh plants can be woven to make baskets, mats, chair seats, and the like.

Did you know?

- The common reed, or phragmites, is considered the world's most abundant plant species. Phragmites spreads by colonizing disturbed land along roadsides, in vacant lots, and almost anywhere humankind has messed up nature.

- Musical instruments such as saxophones, clarinets, oboes, and bassoons are known as reed instruments, or woodwinds, because they use thin slices of bamboo (a reed) to produce their sounds. Other instruments, such as accordions and organs, use similar "reeds" made of metal, plastic, or other materials.

RUSH FLOWER

RUSHES

What's the difference between . . . . Anemones and Sea Anemones?

A world of difference. They belong to different **kingdoms** of living things.

Anemones are flowering plants. Sometimes called windflowers, anemones look a bit like daisies or asters.

Sea anemones are animals. They are related to corals, but they look more like underwater flowers. The "petals" of the sea anemone's "flower" are stinging, food-gathering **tentacles** that surround the creature's mouth.

ANEMONE

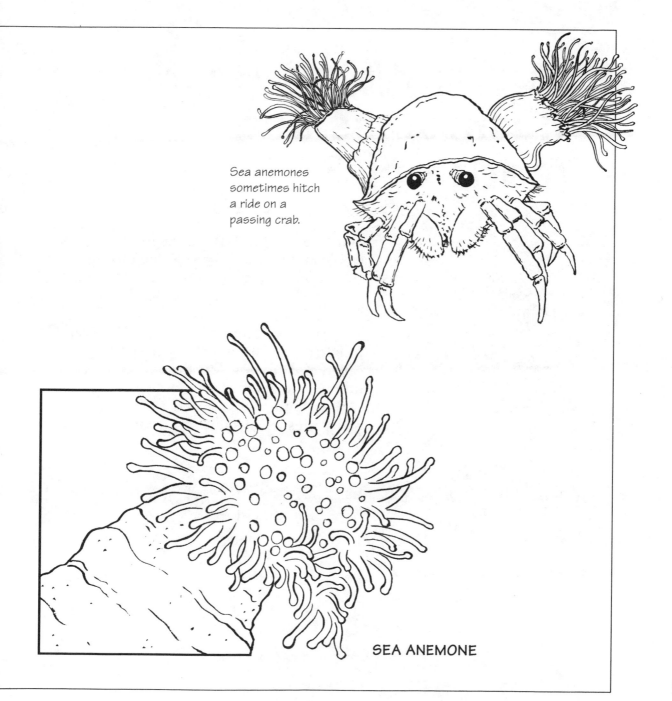

Sea anemones
sometimes hitch
a ride on a
passing crab.

SEA ANEMONE

What's the difference between . . .
Mushrooms and Toadstools?

hen of the woods

Some people think that mushrooms are edible and toadstools are poisonous, but "toadstool" is just another name for "mushroom."

All mushrooms are fungi, but not all fungi are mushrooms. Only fleshy fungi are called mushrooms. Mushrooms aren't all umbrella-shaped either. Some look like sponges, others like corals. The names of many mushrooms tell you what they look

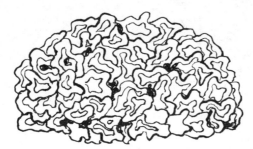

cauliflower fungus

bird's nest fungi

like: horn of plenty, pig's ears, cauliflower fungus, hen of the woods, bird's
nest fungus, earthstar, jelly fungus, dead
man's fingers, scarlet cup, and giant
puffball.

pig's ears

puffballs

Did you know?

- There is no simple way to tell whether a
  mushroom is edible or poisonous. The only
  sure way is to identify the exact species and
  know whether it's safe or good to eat. Some
  mushrooms that are perfectly *safe* to eat taste
  terrible. Never eat a mushroom in the wild
  without asking an adult

- The part of the mushroom we see is just the
  "tip of the iceberg." What we call the mushroom is really only its fruiting body. The rest
  of the mushroom lives under the ground or in
  the rotting wood of a log as a network of
  threads called a **mycelium**.

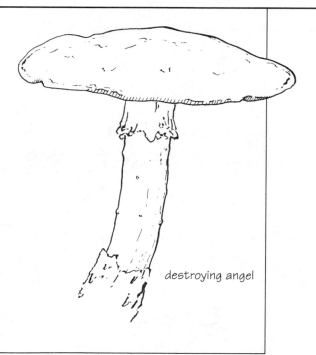

destroying angel

What's the difference between . . .
Mosses and Lichens?

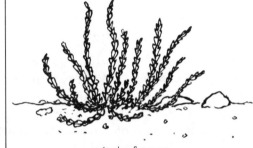

spineleaf moss

Mosses are a special group of primitive plants that lack roots, stems, or veins for moving water around within their leaves. A lichen is actually a tiny "colony" of two plants: a **fungus** and an **alga**.

Lichens are even more primitive than mosses, and can grow in drier places (such

Spanish moss

"MOSSES"

as on bare rocks). Mosses are usually found in damp places. This is because they need to soak up water to survive.

Lichens are an example of a special partnership called a **symbiotic relationship**. The alga uses its chlorophyll to make food for the fungus, which couldn't grow on bare rocks. The fungus uses its fine threads (the mycelium) to capture the water and minerals needed by the alga. Without the one the other would not survive.

Some lichens are edible, but not very tasty. Still, they can be useful in other ways. For example, some lichens are used to make **antibiotics**. Others are used to make dyes.

Many plants that are called mosses aren't really mosses at all. The plant called reindeer moss is actually a lichen. The seaweeds called Irish moss and sea moss are really algae. And Spanish moss is actually a flowering plant, a member of the pineapple family!

LICHENS

What's the difference between . . .
Molds and Mildews?

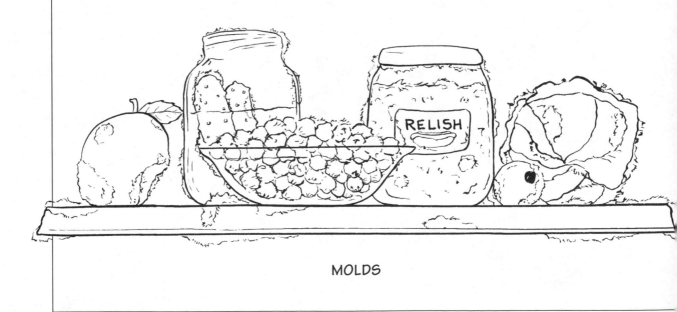

CLOSE-UP OF
MOLD

Molds, the fuzzy, scuzzy things that form on food
that's been kept in the refrigerator too long, come in
many colors: green, blue, white, gray, and black.
Mildews are similar to molds, but are usually white
and form thin, almost powdery coatings on plants,
cloth, paper, and other materials.

RELISH

MOLDS

The color of a mold depends on exactly which type of fungus is involved. (How did it get in the refrigerator? From microscopic spores that settled on the food when it was out in the air. The food nourishes the mold, which grows and grows and grows.)

Both molds and mildews are fungi that form coatings on damp **organic** surfaces. On shower curtains and walls, mildews feed on organic soap scum.

plant with mildew

CLOSE-UP OF MILDEW

MILDEW

Animals

What's the difference between . . .
Apes and Monkeys?

gorilla

Tails. Monkeys have them, apes don't.

Apes and monkeys are almost alike in every other way. Both belong to a larger group of animals called primates. In general, primates have relatively large brains, good eyesight, enlarged thumbs and big toes, and flattened nails rather than claws. Most primates are tree-dwellers and vegetarians.

In addition to having good eyesight, most primates have binocular vision. That doesn't mean

chimpanzee

orangutan

gibbon

APES

Did you know?

- Human beings are also primates.

- Apes and monkeys are also called simians, from a Latin word that means "snub-nosed."

- Many of the most primitive primates—such as lemurs, aye-ayes, lorises, and bushbabies—are endangered because they have been hunted and their rainforest habitats have been destroyed.

- The black lemur is the only primate, other than human beings, that has blue eyes.

- The dwarf lemur is the only primate that hibernates.

their eyes magnify things as binoculars do. It means that their eyes are located on the front of their heads so both eyes can focus on the same thing at the same time. This gives the animal **depth perception**, the ability to judge distances. Imagine trying to leap from branch to branch without it!

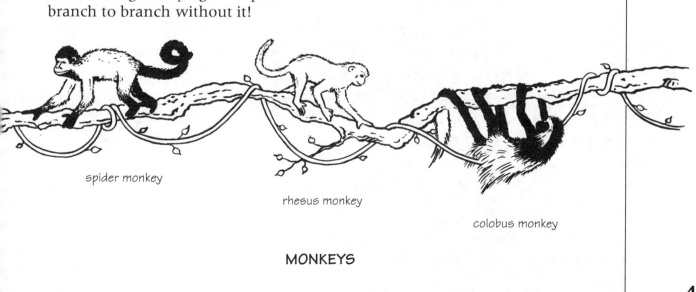

spider monkey

rhesus monkey

colobus monkey

MONKEYS

What's the difference between . . .
Jaguars and Leopards?

Jaguars live in South and Central America and have central spots inside their **rosettes** (which are rings formed by smaller spots). Leopards live in Africa and Asia and have smaller rosettes with no center spots. The jaguar is the only one of the **great cats** that doesn't roar. Instead, it hisses and screams like mountain lions, lynxes, and other smaller cats.

Even though these cats are closely related, there are other differences between them. Jaguars are good swimmers, and can

JAGUAR SPOT

JAGUAR

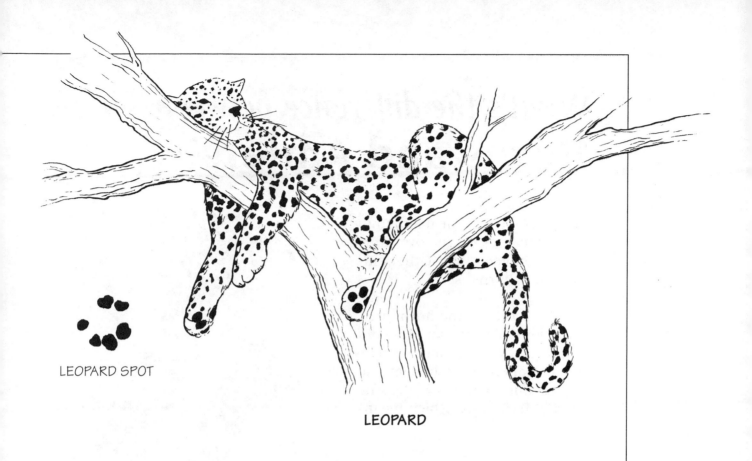

LEOPARD SPOT

LEOPARD

usually be found around rivers. Leop-ards will swim if they have to, but otherwise they don't like to be in the water. The leopard is slender. The jaguar is a stockier animal, with a larger head and heavier jaw.

There is one important similarity between jaguars and leopards. Both are endangered because they have been hunted illegally for their spotted coats.

Did you know?

• Leopards usually visit a water hole daily, but they can go for as much as a month without water.

• Cats are native to all but two continents. Only Antarctica and Australia have no native cats.

• Individual jaguars and leopards can be all black, in which case they are called black panthers.

What's the difference between . . .
Horns and Antlers?

Only members of the deer family, which includes elk, moose, and caribou, have antlers. Other animals have horns.

Both antlers and horns are hard, bony objects that grow out from the head. But horns usually are permanent growths that last throughout an animal's life. Antlers are deciduous, which means

giraffe

Dall sheep

HORNS

they fall off and are regrown each year. Horns have an inner core of bone and an outer layer of a different material, usually **keratin** (the same substance that makes hair, nails, and hooves). Antlers are solid because they are made of the same material inside and out.

white-tailed deer

moose

ANTLERS

Did you know?

- Rhinoceros "horns" aren't really horns, but growths of hard skin.

- Great horned owls, horned larks, horned lizards, horned vipers, and horned sharks don't have horns at all. Their "horns" are just pointed tufts of feathers, skin projections, or spines.

- Pronghorns, which are often mistakenly called pronghorn antelopes, are the only horned animals that shed the outer layers of their horns each year.

- Most horned animals develop their horns as they grow, but baby giraffes are born with theirs. At birth, the baby giraffe's horns are relatively soft and are folded flat against the head.

What's the difference between . . .
Rabbits and Hares?

cottontail

Hares are bigger, have longer legs and ears, and are stronger runners than rabbits. Hares are born with their eyes open, and they are covered with fur. Rabbits are born naked, with closed eyes. Hares can run shortly after they are born. Newborn rabbits are helpless, utterly dependent upon their parents.

RABBITS

Rabbits and hares also have some important behavioral differences. When rabbits want to get out of bad weather, they use burrows, which are holes or tunnels they dig in the ground. Hares seek shelter in scratched-out depressions in the ground, rocky ledges, fallen trees, or hollow cacti. These hare hiding places are called "forms."

Rabbits build fur-lined dens in depressions when it's time to bear their young. Hares simply use the same sheltered forms they use for sleeping.

Did you know?

- Jackrabbits are actually hares, not rabbits.

- Snowshoe hares are white only in wintertime. The rest of the year their coats are brown.

- Rabbits and hares are not rodents. They are called **lagomorphs**. (It's from two Greek words meaning hare-shaped.) The difference between lagomorphs and rodents is in their teeth. Lagomorphs have an extra pair of small **incisors** that don't have cutting edges.

- Only animals that lay eggs have nests. The "nests" of all other animals should be called dens.

jackrabbit

HARES

What's the difference between . . .
Dolphins, Porpoises, and Whales?

Mainly size.

All of these air-breathing marine mammals are whales, or cetaceans. Whales are divided into two groups called toothed whales and baleen whales. The best known of the toothed whales is the sperm whale, which feeds on giant squids and octopuses. The baleen whales include the large, toothless whales that eat **plank-**

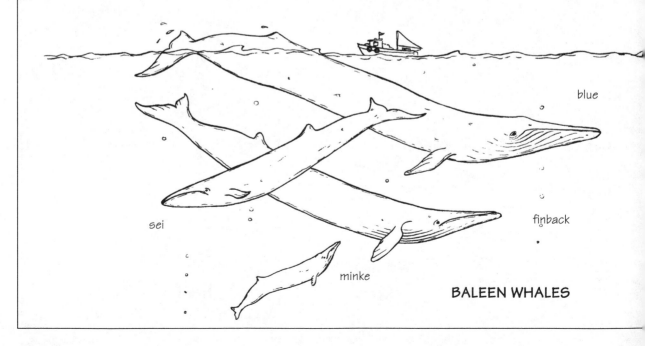

sei

minke

blue

finback

BALEEN WHALES

ton, such as the blue, right, sei, minke, and finback whales.

The smaller toothed whales are usually called dolphins or porpoises. If a small-toothed whale has a beak-shaped mouth, it's usually called a dolphin. If its head is blunt, it's called a porpoise. Sailors usually call all small whales porpoises, and so do some biologists.

Many whale species have been hunted almost to extinction, first for oil, and more recently for human and pet food. Porpoises and dolphins are sometimes killed by fishermen who think they eat too many fish. Sometimes, these smaller cetaceans are killed when

Did you know?

- Cetaceans differ from all other mammals by having neither hair nor hind legs.

- Dolphin is also the name of a fish. To avoid confusion, people often use the fish's Polynesian name, mahi-mahi, or its Spanish name, dorado. In California, fishermen sometimes call it dolphinfish.

they become entangled in the nets fishermen use to catch tuna, salmon, and other fish. That's why you should only eat tuna from cans marked "dolphin safe."

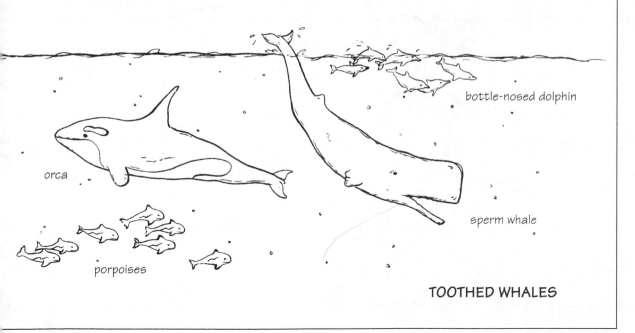

orca

bottle-nosed dolphin

sperm whale

porpoises

TOOTHED WHALES

53

What's the difference between . . .
Seals and Sea Lions?

Sea lions have visible, external ears. Seals don't. And sea lions can turn their rear flippers forward to make walking on land easier. Seals can't, so they have to wriggle their way over the rocks.

SEALS

SEA LIONS

As a group, seals and sea lions are called pinnipeds, which means feather-footed or wing-footed. The third family of pinnipeds, the walruses, have "walking" flippers, like sea lions, but lack external ears, like seals.

The sea lion, or eared seal, family also includes the so-called fur seals, which have external ears and flippers adapted for walking. Perhaps they should be called "fur sea lions."

Did you know?

- The "seals" you see in circuses, aquariums, and zoos are nearly always California sea lions.

- The smallest pinniped, the ringed seal, weighs 200 pounds, while the largest, the southern elephant seal, can weigh as much as 8,000 pounds.

What's *the difference between . . .*
Hair and Fur?

Fur is hair, but hair isn't fur.

Hair is the name given the threadlike stuff that grows from the skin of mammals. It's also the name given to a mammal's hairy coat.

Fur is the name given to the thick coat of an animal that has *soft* hair. It's also the name used to describe the **pelt** of a fur-bearing animal, as well as coats and other things made from those pelts.

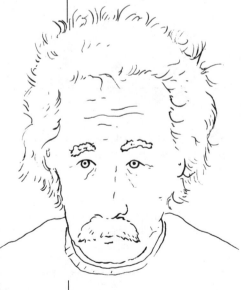

HAIR

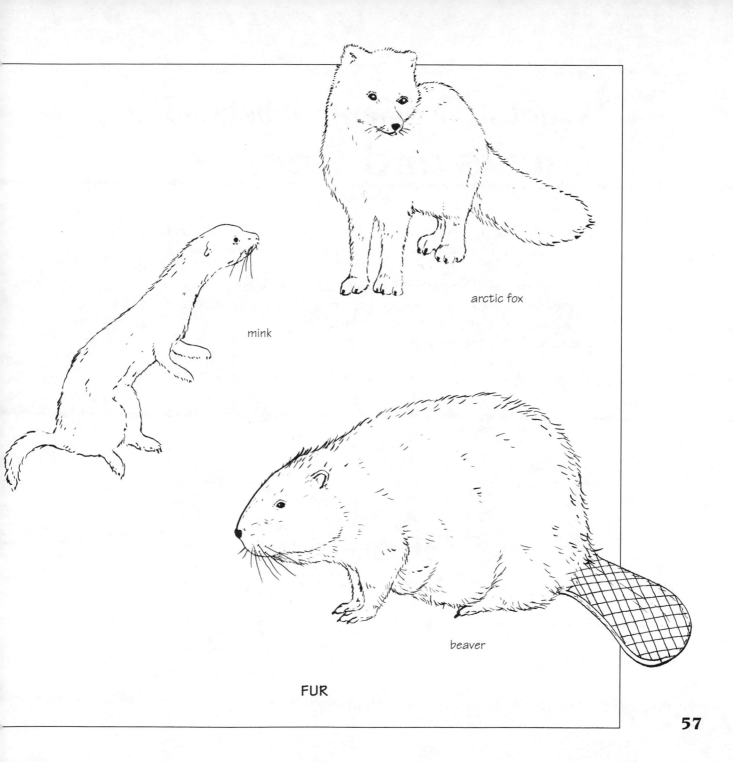

arctic fox

mink

beaver

FUR

What's the difference between . . .
Ducks and Geese?

Size is the big difference between these closely related birds. Ducks are smaller and more slender and have shorter necks than geese.

Of course, there are other differences between ducks and geese. Most geese do as much (or more) of their feeding on land as in water, whereas ducks are primarily water feeders. Geese are primarily

wood ducks

mallard

black duck

pintail

DUCKS

vegetarian, whereas most ducks eat both plant and animal food.

Ducks are sometimes divided into divers and dabblers. Diving ducks go deep under water for their food; dabbling ducks usually feed in shallower water, tipping up and down. Dabblers have larger wings and can take off vertically. Because of their smaller wings, divers have to splash along the surface to get airborne. Most dabbling ducks live in freshwater; many diving ducks are sea ducks.

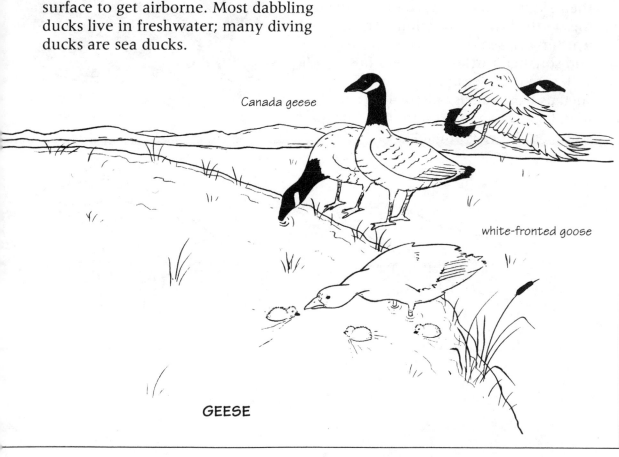

Canada geese

white-fronted goose

GEESE

59

What's the difference between . . .
Reptiles and Amphibians?

Reptiles—which include snakes, lizards, turtles, and crocodilians—have scales, shields, or plates covering their skins, and the legged ones have toes with claws. (Exceptions: The leatherback sea turtle has no claws, and softshell turtles have very few scales on their legs.) Amphibians—such as frogs, toads, and salamanders—have moist skin without scales, and toes without claws.

timber rattlesnake

green anole

tortoise

REPTILES

There are other important differences. Amphibians pass through a **larval** stage before becoming adults (for example, tadpoles are the larvae of frogs). Because of this, amphibians must live near water. Young reptiles, on the other hand, are miniature versions of the adults and can live in deserts and other dry places. Amphibians have toes without claws.

Did you know?

- The so-called glass snake is actually a legless lizard. You can tell it isn't a snake because it has movable eyelids and external ear openings. Snakes lack these features.

- The Florida worm lizard also looks a bit like a snake, and a lot like an earthworm, but it's not a snake, a lizard, or a worm. It belongs to a strange group of reptiles called amphisbaenias (AM-fizz-BEAN-ee-yas). Like other reptiles, it has scales, but they are arranged in rings that resemble the earthworm's segments. The worm lizard also lacks both external ear openings and external eyes.

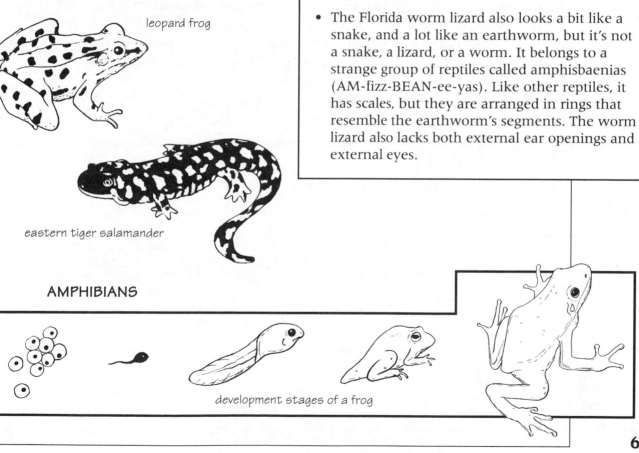

leopard frog

eastern tiger salamander

AMPHIBIANS

development stages of a frog

What's the difference between . . . Newts and Salamanders?

Newts are salamanders, but not all salamanders are newts.

There are exceptions to these rules, but there are several reasons why newts are given their own corner of the salamander world.

The important difference—the one that scientists use—involves the teeth that grow out of the **palates** in their mouths. Most sala-

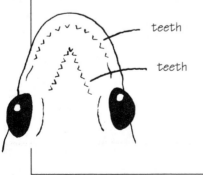

teeth

teeth

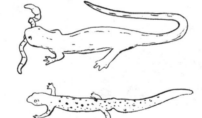

rough-skinned newt

Eastern newt

black spotted newt

red-bellied newt

NEWTS

manders have palatal teeth arranged in two side-by-side arcs; a newt's are in two rows that almost form a vee.

Also, most salamanders have prominent grooves along their sides, between their front and rear legs; newts don't. Salamanders may live on land or in the water; newts are creatures of the water. Most salamanders have smooth, slippery (even slimy) skins that make them difficult to hold onto. And adult newts have skins that are rougher than a salamander's.

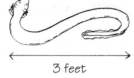

Did you know?

- The giant Japanese salamander grows as long as 5 feet. The largest American salamander, the greater siren, can be more than 3 feet (1 meter) long. Even the dwarf siren gets pretty big: 10 inches (25 centimeters).

  3 feet

- The small, red-orange "salamanders" found in eastern woodlands are a land-dwelling stage of certain newts. They are called "efts."

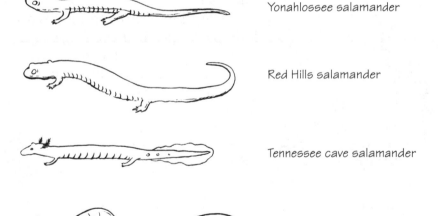

Yonahlossee salamander

Red Hills salamander

Tennessee cave salamander

California slender salamander

SALAMANDERS

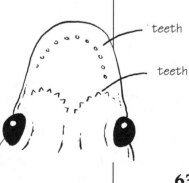

teeth

teeth

What's the difference between . . .
Frogs and Toads?

Frogs and toads are both amphibians, but check their skin. If the skin is smooth and moist, it's probably a frog. If the skin is dry and warty, you can bet it's a toad.

Okay, there are exceptions. A few frogs have warts. The Colorado River toad has moist skin. But there are other differences between frogs and toads.

Both have short front legs and long back legs. But the frog's back legs are r-e-a-a-a-l-l-y long. The toad's are meant for hopping; the frog's, for leaping.

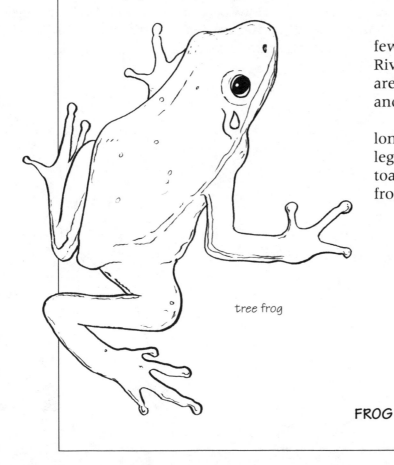

tree frog

FROG

Frogs have ridges running down the edges of their backs (except for the bullfrog, whose ridges stop right above the front legs).

Frogs have tiny upper teeth, but toads are toothless.

Frogs are often found in and around water, whereas toads are land creatures. However, many toads lay their eggs in water.

Actually, there are so many exceptions to these differences, scientists have pretty much given up trying to distinguish between frogs and toads. Some scientists just call them all frogs.

Did you know?

- The wood frog's range extends all the way up into Arctic Canada and Alaska. It has the northernmost range of all North American reptiles and amphibians. Imagine, hibernating all winter in **permafrost**!

- People get warts from handling toads about as frequently as frogs turn into princes when they are kissed. But it's still a good idea to wash your hands after handling a toad. This won't prevent warts, but it will prevent its skin secretions from irritating your eyes or mouth. Some toads even have poison glands in their skin to protect them from predators.

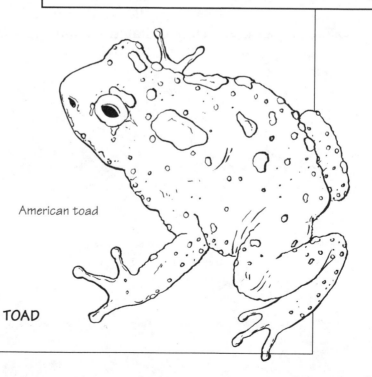

American toad

TOAD

What's the difference between . . .
Alligators and Crocodiles?

Alligators have very broad, rounded snouts. Crocodiles have narrower snouts. When a crocodile's jaws are closed, the large fourth teeth in its lower jaw are exposed. When an alligator closes its jaws, you can't see its lower teeth.

There are 21 species of large, armored reptiles called crocodilians: 2 alligators, 12 crocodiles, 5 caimans, and 2 garials. In the United States, we have just 2 native species: the American alligator and the American crocodile.

ALLIGATORS

CROCODILES

Caimans are closely related to alligators. But caimans have sharper snouts, and their bellies are "armor" plated. An alligator's belly isn't much tougher than a large lizard's. Caimans are native to Central and South America.

Garials (also called gavials) have extremely long, slender snouts with enlarged tips and fierce-looking teeth. They live in India and other parts of southern Asia.

Did you know?

• Alligators and crocodiles can run almost as fast as horses for short distances. To escape danger, or to attack, they can raise their big bodies up on their short legs and make like sprinters.

What's *the difference between . . .*
Turtles, Tortoises, and Terrapins?

Not much. Turtles, tortoises, and terrapins are very much alike.

Some people think that only the land-dwelling turtles should be called tortoises. They also think that the name "turtle" should only be used for those turtles that spend much of their time in or around water. Some even suggest that the name "terrapin" (a Native American word) should only be used for turtles that divide their time between land and water. But everyone else seems to agree that it's correct to call all three of these creatures turtles.

spotted turtles

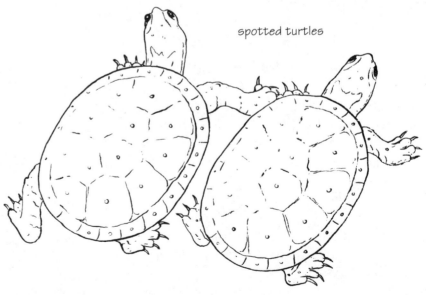

loggerhead

giant tortoises

snapping turtle

Did you know?

- Both the largest and the smallest turtles are called tortoises. The 4½-foot-long Galapagos tortoise is the world's largest turtle, and the 4-inch-long speckled tortoise is the smallest.

A sea turtle hatching.

What's the difference between . . .
Skates and Stingrays?

Skates have fins and thick tails, but never barbed spines. Stingrays have long, skinny, whiplike tails with the barbed spines that give them their name. Most stingrays do not have tail fins.

Skates and stingrays are the two largest families of rays. Rays are distant cousins of sharks with large, winglike pectoral fins. Like most rays, skates and stingrays are bottom-dwellers that spend a lot of time buried in the sand.

There are many other kinds of rays. Some of these are:

- Guitarfishes, which look almost like a cross between skates and angel sharks.

- Sawfishes, which are large rays that have a projection from the head that looks like a chain saw.

- Torpedoes, or electric rays, which lack the stingray's weaponry, but have one of their own: electric organs on either side of the head.

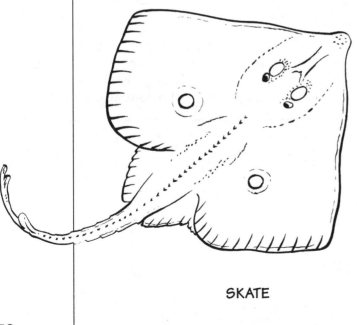

SKATE

These can produce an electric current (up to 220 volts) that will discourage anything that bites, grabs, or steps on it.

Did you know?

- All skates are good to eat. So are sawfishes and guitarfishes and some other rays.

- Mantas, which are huge rays with horns that project from their heads. (The "horns" are really specialized fins that can be used like scoops as the mantas swim through schools of fish.) Mantas have long, whiplike tails, but only a few of them have spines. The Atlantic manta may measure as much as 22 feet across from one pointed "wingtip" to the other. Mantas and eagle rays are strong, free swimmers that travel great distances.

STINGRAY

What's the difference between . . .
Bone and Cartilage?

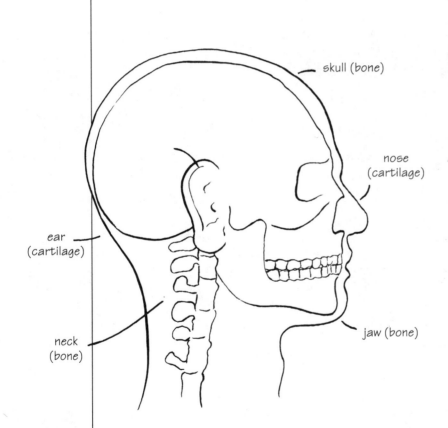

skull (bone)

nose
(cartilage)

ear
(cartilage)

neck
(bone)

jaw (bone)

Bone is the special tissue that the skeletons of most higher animals are made of. Cartilage is similar to bone, but softer, more flexible, and more **translucent** (which means it's easier to see light through) than bone. In most animal joints and spines, cartilage acts as a cushion between the moving bones. Without it, the bones would grind each other away.

Bone is very complicated stuff. At its center is soft bone marrow. The outer portions of bone tissue are nonliving. The living bone cells there have been replaced by calcium and phosphorus. Within the hard bone there are lots of tiny spaces where bone cells can live. Many blood vessels flow through these living bone tissues.

In adult animals, cartilage does not contain blood vessels. In very young animals, much of the cartilage has blood vessels, but most of that cartilage turns into bone as the animal grows.

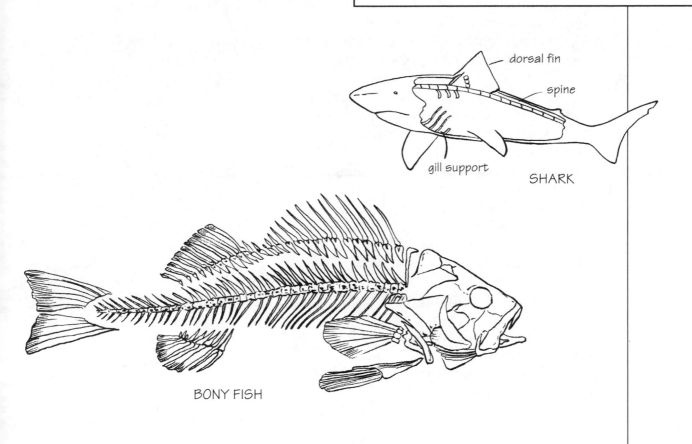

Did you know?

- Sharks, skates, rays, sturgeons, and a few other fish relatives have no bone in their skeletons, just cartilage.

- The end of your nose and the outer edges of your ears are made of cartilage, not bone.

dorsal fin

spine

gill support

SHARK

BONY FISH

What's the difference between . . .
Octopuses and Squids?

Octopuses have eight arms. Squids also have eight arms (which are usually much shorter than an octopus's), but they also have two long **tentacles**. Unlike arms, which have suckers their entire length, tentacles have suckers only on their clublike ends.

Octopuses have short, thick, saclike bodies, called mantles. Octopuses have no fins, and their arms are connected to their mantles by what looks like a web of skin. Squids have longer, narrower mantles with fins. Unlike octopuses, squids don't have a weblike piece of skin between the bases of the arms.

Octopuses, squids, and their closest relatives are all called cephalopods (which means head-footed). Cephalopods range from less than an inch to more

OCTOPUS

than 60 feet in length. The other cephalopods share some features with octopuses and squids, but also have some of their own.

Cuttlefish have fins, like squids. But their bodies are shaped more like an octopus's. Cuttlefish also have two tentacles in addition to eight arms. Unlike the squid's, the cuttlefish's tentacles can be retracted into pockets. And cuttlefish have eyelids on their eyes, which neither squids nor octopuses do.

Nautiluses live inside shells. The nautilus's arms are short, but it may have as many as 94 of them!

Although cephalopods are usually considered primitive animals, they are amazingly intelligent. Octopuses are probably the smartest of the cephalopods and the fastest learners. Squids seem to have more methods of communication with one another. Cuttlefish are even more "talkative" than squids. Nautiluses aren't as smart or as communicative as their cephalopod cousins.

SQUIDS

Did you know?
• Cephalopods range from less than an inch to more than 60 feet in length.

What's *the difference between . . .*
Butterflies and Moths?

The most important difference between butterflies and moths is their antennae. Butterfly antennae usually have a clublike swelling on the end. Moth antennae are usually feathery or threadlike.

Even though they're closely related, butterflies and moths differ in several ways. Butterflies are day-flying insects with slender bodies and broad, usually brilliantly colored wings. Moths are active at nightfall or after dark and have broader bodies and proportionally smaller wings than butterflies. Moths are usually less brilliantly colored than butterflies, too.

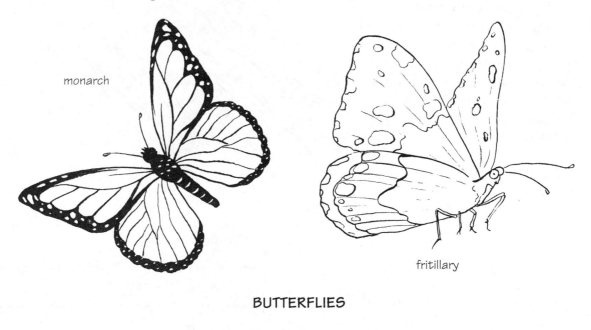

monarch

fritillary

BUTTERFLIES

Even at a distance, you can tell moths and butterflies apart when they fly. Moths have much faster wing beats. Butterflies sail a lot between wing beats.

Naturally, there are plenty of exceptions. Some butterflies, such as the brown wood nymphs or satyrs, are quite drab compared to royal moths, which are brightly patterned in reds, pinks, yellows, and browns. And few butterflies are more spectacularly colored than the luna moth, which has huge wings.

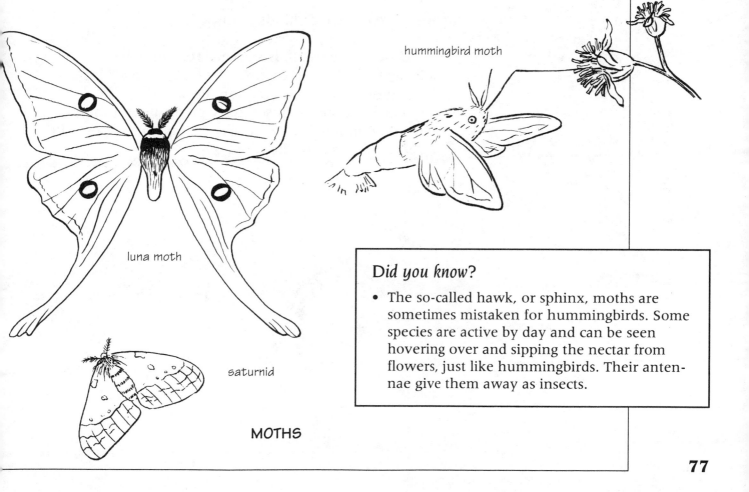

hummingbird moth

luna moth

saturnid

MOTHS

Did you know?

- The so-called hawk, or sphinx, moths are sometimes mistaken for hummingbirds. Some species are active by day and can be seen hovering over and sipping the nectar from flowers, just like hummingbirds. Their antennae give them away as insects.

What's the difference between . . .
Bugs and Insects?

Bugs are particular kinds of insects.

Insects are small, **invertebrate** animals with jointed bodies and six jointed legs. The typical insect has a mouth with jaws that are designed for biting and chewing. Flies, mosquitoes, gnats, bees, moths, ants, dragonflies, mayflies, beetles, and crickets are all insects, but none of them is a bug.

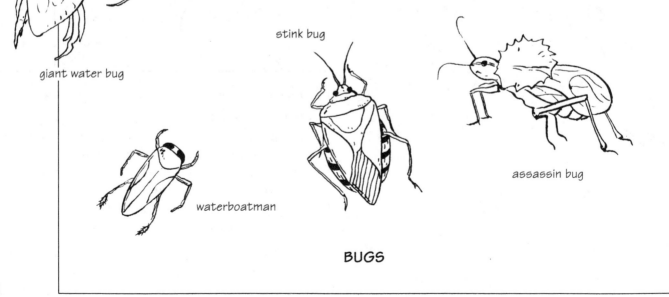

giant water bug

stink bug

waterboatman

assassin bug

BUGS

A bug has a long, pointed tube for a mouth. It stabs its beak into plants (and sometimes, animals) and sucks their juices. Bugs also have front wings that are thick near the bug's body and thin and transparent at the tip. Stink bugs, lace bugs, water bugs, and water scorpions are examples of bugs.

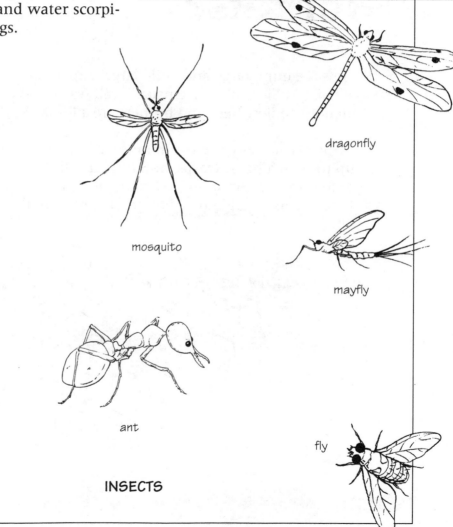

Did you know?

- Spiders aren't insects. Spiders have eight legs and belong to a class of invertebrate animals called **arachnids**.

dragonfly

mosquito

mayfly

gnat

ant

fly

INSECTS

What's the difference between . . .
Bees, Wasps, and Hornets?

Hornets are quite large and build large, papery nests. Bees often have hairy bodies. What we usually call wasps have shiny, deeply segmented bodies. Bees and hornets are a lot fatter than wasps.

Wasp is actually the common name for the very large insect group to which bees, wasps, and hornets all belong. Wasps have these features in common: two pairs of wings, a segmented body in three sections, and jaws that are made for both chewing and sucking.

BEES

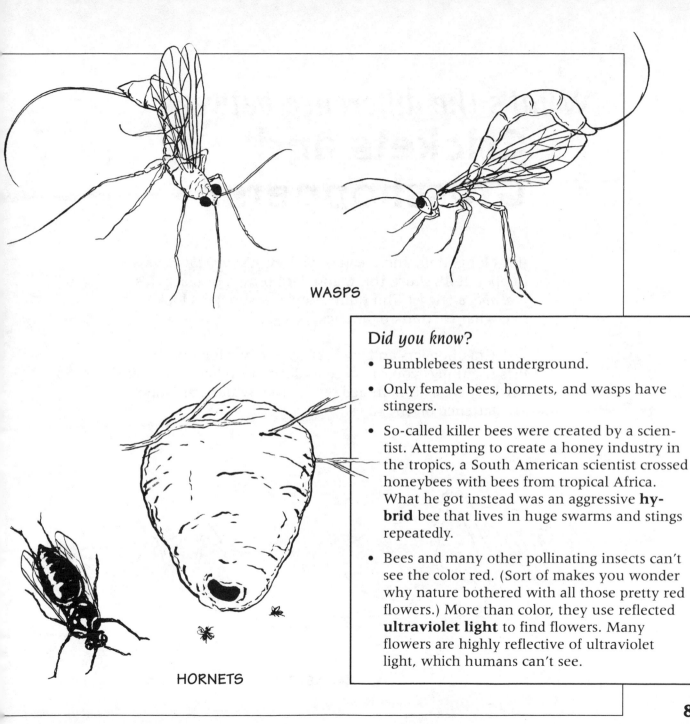

WASPS

HORNETS

Did you know?

- Bumblebees nest underground.

- Only female bees, hornets, and wasps have stingers.

- So-called killer bees were created by a scientist. Attempting to create a honey industry in the tropics, a South American scientist crossed honeybees with bees from tropical Africa. What he got instead was an aggressive **hybrid** bee that lives in huge swarms and stings repeatedly.

- Bees and many other pollinating insects can't see the color red. (Sort of makes you wonder why nature bothered with all those pretty red flowers.) More than color, they use reflected **ultraviolet light** to find flowers. Many flowers are highly reflective of ultraviolet light, which humans can't see.

81

What's the difference between . . .
Crickets and Grasshoppers?

If it's long, thin, and green or yellow, it's *probably* a grass-hopper. If it's short, thick, and dark brown or black, it's *probably* a cricket. But quite a few grasshoppers look more like what we think of as crickets.

Grasshoppers and crickets are really a lot alike. Scientists use things you can't see to distinguish between them. Crickets are a bit flattened on the top, while grasshoppers are flattened on the sides.

field crickets

cave cricket

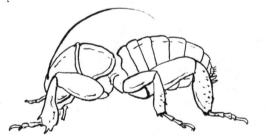

Jerusalem cricket

CRICKETS

Crickets have the reputation for singing the summer nights away by sawing one wing against the other. But many grasshoppers also add their "voices" to the nightly summer chorus.

Did you know?

- Usually only the males sing. Females of a few species can make sounds, but they are soft sounds.

- The nearest relatives of grasshoppers and crickets are katydids, praying mantises, walkingsticks, and cockroaches.

GRASSHOPPER

Glossary

These brief and simple definitions are meant to help you read and understand this book. They are not complete definitions of the words and terms listed. Please use a dictionary or encyclopedia to find out more about these things.

alga, algae   *Alga* is singular, *algae* is plural. Algae make up one of the largest groups of living things. The smallest algae are tiny, almost microscopic, one-celled organisms. The largest is the giant kelp that grows in huge, underwater "forests" off the coast of California. Single-celled algae may not have chlorophyll, cell walls, and some of the other features that define plants. For this reason, many scientists place algae in the Protist or Monera Kingdoms.

anther   Part of a flower that produces the pollen that fertilizes the female organs.

antibiotics   Medicines made from living organisms, such as fungi and lichens, which kill bacteria and other disease microorganisms. Penicillin was the first of the so-called "wonder drugs." It was made from a fungus called *Penicillium*.

arachnid   An invertebrate animal with eight legs, such as spiders, scorpions, or horseshoe crabs.

bronchial   Of or relating to the bronchus or other parts of the bronchial system. The bronchus is the main "windpipe" leading into the lungs.

chlorophyll   The name given to a group of green substances found in plants. Chlorophyll uses the sun's energy, carbon dioxide, and water to produce carbohydrates. Carbohydrates are the high-energy foods in our diets, such as starches and sugars.

deciduous   Falling off. Anything that is periodically shed (such as the leaves of trees or the antlers of deer) is said to be deciduous.

depth perception   The ability to judge how far away an object is. When two eyes focus on the same object, each eye sees the object differently. The brain uses this information to judge distances. Only animals that have two eyes on the front of the head have this ability.

fungi, fungus   *Fungi* is plural, *fungus* is singular. The best known fungi are mushrooms. (See *What is the difference between mushrooms and toadstools?*) Other fungi include molds and mildews. Fungi lack chlorophyll and are parasitic (which means they live off decaying matter). Once considered plants, fungi now have their own kingdom.

great cats   The four largest members of the cat family: lion, tiger, leopard, and jaguar. All but the jaguar can roar, which smaller cats can't do.

hybrid   The offspring of parents of different species or breeds. Some hybrids occur in nature, but most are the result of human planning. Most of our food crops and ornamental plants are hybrids that were intentionally crossbred to produce plants that are bigger, hardier, prettier, tastier, or in some way "better" than the originals.

hydra   Small, tube-shaped freshwater animal related to jellyfish. At one end of the tube is a mouth, surrounded by tentacles that capture food.

incisor   A cutting tooth, such as one of your front teeth.

invertebrate   Lacking a spine or backbone. Invertebrate animals include insects and shellfish. Animals with spines are called **vertebrates**.

keratin   The name given to a variety of compounds that form hair, nails, feathers, horns, and other tissues that grow out of the skin of animals.

kingdom   The major divisions of living things. Once there were just two kingdoms: Plant and Animal. Now there are five: Plant, Animal, Fungi, Protist, and Monera.

lagomorph   The name (meaning hare-shaped) given to the order of gnawing animals that includes hares, rabbits, and pikas.

larva, larval   *Larval* is the adjective form of *larva*. A larva is an early form of any animal that at birth is very different from its parents. A frog's larva, called a tadpole, has a tail but no legs. Many flying insects have a wingless, wormlike larval stage.

Monera Kingdom   One of the five kingdoms of living things. The Monera Kingdom includes primitive, one-celled bacteria and blue-green algae. Some monerans use chlorophyll to make their own food, and were once considered plants. But, unlike those of plants, moneran cells do not contain nuclei.

mycelium   The usually unnoticed mass of threadlike fibers that make up the vegetative (nonreproductive) body of a fungus. What we call a mushroom is the fruiting (reproductive) body of the fungus.

nonvascular   Not having the tubes or channels that transport the body fluids in animals and vascular plants.

organic   Of, relating to, or obtained from living things. Coal is not alive, but it is organic because it is made of decayed plant matter. All organic substances contain carbon.

ovary   The reproductive part of a flower containing **ovules**.

ovule   In seed plants, the part of the ovary that develops into a seed.

palate   The roof of the mouth separating the mouth from the nasal cavity in the head.

pelt   The skin of an animal, including its hair, wool, or fur.

permafrost   A permanently frozen layer in the ground. In polar regions, it may be at or just below the surface, even in the hottest part of the summer.

pistil (or **carpel**)   The female reproductive organ of a flower.

plankton   Floating plant or animal life in a body of water. Plant plankton is called phytoplankton. Animal plankton is called zooplankton. An individual member of the plankton community is a plankter. Some animal plankters are weak swimmers, but most drift with the currents.

Protist Kingdom   One of the five kingdoms of living things. The Protist Kingdom is made up of one-celled or noncellular organisms that do not fit the definitions for plants or animals. Certain algae, protozoans, amoebas, bacteria, and sometimes viruses are now classified in the Protist Kingdom.

rosette   A design or pattern in the shape of a rose.

stamen   The male reproductive organ of a flower.

stigma   The part of a flower that collects the pollen. It is located at the top of the **pistil**.

symbiotic relationship   The relationship of two different organisms that live together, especially when the relationship is helpful to both.

symmetrical   Having the same size, shape, or parts on either side of a dividing line through the middle. People are symmetrical left to right, but not top to bottom. Flowers such as daisies are symmetrical in all directions.

tentacle   A long, flexible, armlike structure on an animal. Tentacles are used in feeling, grasping, or moving. In many animals, tentacles are located around or near the mouth and are used to gather food.

translucent   Permitting the passage of diffused light. Objects viewed through translucent materials cannot be seen clearly.

transparent   Permitting the passage of undiffused light. Objects viewed through transparent material can be seen clearly.

ultraviolet light   Invisible part of the light spectrum. Ultraviolet light is located on the shortwave end of the light spectrum. Ultraviolet light is also called UV or black light.

vascular   Having tubes or channels that carry body fluids, such as blood in animals or sap in plants.

vertebrate   Having a spine or backbone. Fish, reptiles, amphibians, birds, and mammals are vertebrates. (See also **invertebrate**.)

Index

alga, algae, vii, viii, 38
amphisbaenias, 61
Animal Kingdom, vii
antennae, 76, 77
anther, 4
antibiotics, 39
arachnids, 79
asexual reproduction, 7
asparagus, 31
aye-aye, 45

bamboo, 3
bee orchids, 5
binocular vision, 44–45
black panthers, 47
bristlecone pine, 19
bronchial tissue, 23
burrows, 51

caimans, 66–67
canes, 3
carpel, 5
cephalopods, 74–75
cereal grains, 3
cetaceans, 52, 53
chlorophyll, vii, viii, 12
cotyledons, 13
cuttlefish, 75

deciduous, 17, 48–49
dens, 51
depth perception, 45
dolphinfish, 53

efts, 63
endangered species, 45, 47
evergreen plants, 17

flowering plants, 4
forms, 51
Fungi Kingdom, viii
fungus, fungi, vii, 31, 36, 38, 41

garials, 66–67
General Grant Tree, 19
General Sherman Tree, 19
giraffe, 48, 49
glass snake, 61
great cats, 46
guitarfishes, 70, 71

hay fever, 22–23
hybrid, 81
hydra, vii

incisors, 51
invertebrates, 78

junipers, 17

keratin, 49
Kingdoms, 34
    Animal, vii
    Fungi, viii
    Monera, viii
    Plant, vii
    Protist, viii

lagomorphs, 51
larches, 17
larva, larvae, 61
legumes, 27
lemurs, 45
lorises, 45

mantas, 71
mergansers, 59
mimosa tree, vii
Monera Kingdom, viii
musical instruments, as reeds, 33
mycelium, 37, 39

nautilus, 75
nectar, 9
nectary, 9
nests, 51, 80, 81
nonvascular, 10

organic, 41
ovary, 5, 24, 25, 31
ovules, 5, 85

palatal teeth, 62–63
peduncle, 11
pelt, 56
permafrost, 65
phragmites, 33
pinnipeds, 55
pistil, 5
plankton, 52–53
Plant Kingdom, vii
plant reproduction, 4–5, 6–7, 8–9, 29, 31
primates, 44–45
pronghorns, 49
Protist Kingdom, viii

rosettes, 46, 86

satyrs, 77
sawfishes, 70, 71
sego lily, 31
sexual reproduction, 7
showy flowers, 4
simians, 45
sirens, 63
sorghum, 3
stamen, 4, 6, 31
stigma, 5
sugarcane, 3
sweet potatoes, 29
symbiotic relationship, 39
symmetrical, 30

tamaracks, 17
tentacles, 34, 74
torpedoes (electric rays), 70
translucent, 72
tuna, 53

ultraviolet light, 81

vascular, 10
vegetables, 25
viruses, viii

warts, 65
watermelon, 25
wood nymphs, 77
worm lizard, 61

yams, 29
yews, 16